A GUIDE TO HELP Y(

One Hundred "I Wills"

After You Say "I Do"

Lissa Noel

One Hundred "I Wills" After I Do © 2021, Lissa J. Noel

All rights reserved. No part of this book may be reproduced without the express, written consent of the author, except in the case of brief quotations embodied in critical articles and reviews.

ISBN:

Revised Edition

Front cover design by Carroll Chiles Moore
Interior design by Sinclair Rishel
Cover photo by Sélavie Photography

Printed in the United States of America

For additional copies of this book or to contact Lissa Noel, email 100iwills@bellsouth.net

This book is dedicated to
my True Source of love and encouragement.

And to Randy, who chooses to love me
even when I don't practice these "I Wills."

Introduction

On the day after you say, "I do," you believe you are going to live happily ever after. Soon the reality of ever after creeps in and you realize that this marriage business is going to involve work… Yes, real effort to keep your love alive.

When my husband and I married 43 years ago, I was determined to keep our love not just alive, but flourishing. I began keeping notes from sermons, books, articles, and lectures. Gathering this wisdom encouraged me to set goals and strategies for dealing with my evolving marriage in a world full of challenges and distractions.

Once our children were almost grown, I decided to get serious about compiling the lessons that have worked best for us. My hope is that this rewarding labor of love for me will bring insight and a more abundant marriage for you.

If you are willing to be challenged and enriched by making your marriage a priority, I suggest trying one "I Will" from this book, and if you see a positive result, try another. Some will be harder to accomplish than others, but an attitude of giving it your best is often contagious.

Life is a journey, and marriage is a significant part of that journey. I am firmly convinced that investing in your marriage can reap lasting dividends for you, your spouse, and your children. Join me as we work each day to make the journey a remarkable one. Together, let's practice 100 "I Wills" after you say, "I do."

I'm cheering for you,
Lissa

Tips to Put the "I Wills" into Practice

Keep your book in a place where it can be seen and used frequently. Try your bedside table, desk, or a favorite chair.

Focus on a few "I Wills" at a time until you see progress. Don't be overwhelmed by reading the entire book and trying to put all of them into practice at once.

Use this as a workbook, making notes, and listing ways to implement the "I Wills" in your marriage. You might want to record some of your goals and successes or even add some of your own "I Wills" in the blank pages at the back of the book.

Concentrate on where you need improvement. Reading with the intent to change your spouse can be counterproductive and frustrating for both of you. Instead, encourage your spouse by letting them know which of the "I Wills" they already demonstrate, and compliment them when they display real effort to implement an "I Will."

Be encouraged. Small changes can produce big results.

TABLE OF CONTENTS

BASICS 11
COMMUNICATION 63
INTIMACY 97
NOTES 118
ACKNOWLEDGMENTS 125
A NOTE ABOUT THE COVER 127

The Basics

1

I will

remember that marriage can be difficult because life can be difficult.

Be encouraged. Most of the challenges you will face are normal, and you can work through them.

2

I will

choose each day to love my spouse.

Marriage is commitment;
love is a decision.

3

I will

be grateful for
my spouse as God's
gift to me.

Your marriage is meant to reflect God's love
and commitment to you.

4

I will

make it a priority to nurture our relationship for the good of each other and for our legacy.

By showing affection, loyalty, and even how to disagree without fighting, you are modeling how to be loving spouses.

5

I will

recognize and remind myself that money will never make us truly rich.

Invest in faith, family, and friends for true happiness.

6

I will

show respect and esteem for my spouse in front of others.

Be your spouse's biggest fan, and keep disagreements, complaints, and sensitive matters private.

7

I will

have an understanding of the economic system in which my spouse was raised.

This helps as you try to blend your money values and financial philosophy.

8

I will

embrace my spouse's family and honor them as my own.

Criticizing your spouse's family is criticizing a part of your spouse.

9

I will

observe the principles God has given to us for the wise use of money.

Recognize that lifestyles of overspending or living in debt are usually signs of deeper issues.

10

I will

ask myself, "Am I treating my spouse like my closest friends?"

Remember how you felt when you said your marriage vows.

11

I will

adopt a balanced schedule that meets the needs of my spouse and family.

Honor your marriage by not over-committing yourself. Try to limit personal, social, and work-related calls when you are having leisure time together.

12

I will

learn to express my love in gifts that my spouse enjoys most.

Give what your spouse wants, instead of what you want your spouse to have. This could be the gift of affection, service, presence, or presents.

13

I will

learn from trusted advisors about money management, investments, insurance, loans, and savings.

The more you both know, the better.

14

I will

be a teammate, not an opponent.

Marriage is cooperation,
not competition.

15

I will

ask myself periodically, "How enjoyable am I to live with?"

Try to see yourself through your spouse's eyes.

16

I will

avoid daydreaming or fantasizing about what I wish my spouse could be or do for me.

Disappointment from uncommunicated expectations can send bad signals toward your innocent spouse.

17

I will

realize that there is not always a right or wrong way to do a project.

As long as the job is accomplished, it doesn't have to necessarily be done your way.

18

I will

resist comparing another's
spouse or marriage
to my own.

The grass is seldom greener on the other side.

19

I will

trust God's timing.

God is always ahead of you.

20

I will

respect my spouse's growth as an individual.

It's normal to grow and change as you
go through different seasons in life.

21

I will

strive to be content with the material possessions we have.

Learn to recognize the difference between basic needs (shelter) and wants (material possessions).

22

I will

work with my spouse to create a realistic financial plan.

Financial discord can be a terrible strain on your marriage.

23

I will

strive to make my spouse feel appreciated, approved of, and admired.

These essential needs will be fulfilled somewhere.

24

I will

commit to our marriage vows.

Considering divorce as an option distracts from daily commitment.

25

I will

build relationships with older couples who model healthy marriages.

Seek mentors, and profit from their wisdom.

26

I will

continually examine my attitude to see if it is helping or hurting our relationship.

Your disposition will almost always rub off on your spouse.

27

I will

appreciate the good in my spouse.

Learn to dismiss critical thoughts
and focus on the positive.

28

I will

pray for and with my spouse.

The statistics for divorce improve dramatically among those couples who pray together.

29

I will

ask myself, "Am I making my spouse feel more important than my family, friends, work, or activities?"

Making your spouse a priority sends a message of love and commitment.

30

I will

strive to be a good steward of our money.

It's good to allow at least twenty-four hours before making significant financial decisions or purchases. If you do buy on impulse, keep receipts and the price tags attached until you are sure.

31

I will

keep trivial marital issues in perspective.

There are a multitude of extreme
adversities in our broken world.

32

I will

choose to be hopeful about
the future of my marriage.

Positive feelings usually follow
positive thoughts.

33

I will

strive to keep my marriage vows fresh.

Examples could be holding hands during the vows at another's wedding or restating your own vows on special anniversaries.

34

I will

be appreciative for the gifts
my spouse has chosen
for me.

Returning presents and being too picky
dampens the joy of gift giving.

35

I will

focus on changing myself, rather than my spouse, to improve our marriage.

Working on your attitude or habits can set an example and can prompt similar responses from your spouse.

36

I will

nurture and express feelings of respect for my spouse's contributions to the family.

For example, if one spouse is working at home with the kids, make sure you validate that choice as a significant career.

37

I will

demonstrate that
love is action.

Sometimes, cooking a meal or doing a chore
can say, "I love you," better than words.

38

I will

agree with my spouse on a spending limit when we are using our combined incomes.

Anything above the limit should be discussed and agreed upon by both of you.

39

I will

recognize my spouse's need for time alone or with others.

We all need space. Too much togetherness can strain even good marriages.

40

I will

foster common interests, activities, and friendships as a couple.

Shared experiences with your spouse
help keep you unified.

41

I will

make our home a loving environment and a place of refuge.

You wouldn't want to dread coming home, would you?

42

I will

establish a habit of getting enough rest.

Exhaustion of mind, body, or spirit are obstacles to intimacy, communication, and abundant living.

43

I will

pay my credit card balance in full each month.

Paying interest is a dangerous habit and a waste of your family resources.

44

I will

minister to my spouse's need for security and significance.

But realize that human love can only add to the basic needs first met by God.

45

I will

keep my promises.

Strive to be trustworthy.

46

I will

be committed to spiritual growth individually and as a couple.

Daily, you are either growing or drifting.

47

I will

strive to accept my spouse
the way they are.

Let the small stuff go, and just love.

48

I will

seek qualified marriage counseling if problems persist without improvement.

Admitting you don't have all the answers will allow you and your spouse to work together towards a solution.

49

I will

take care of my health so that we can enjoy our later years together.

Healthy eating, regular exercise, and medical checkups are important for the long run.

50

I will

understand that none of my earthly relationships will fully satisfy my deepest need to be loved.

Only God's love is constant and unconditional.

51

I will

strive daily to be kind.

Kindness communicates value and respect.

COMMUNICATION

52

I will

encourage my spouse.

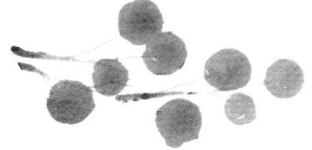

Encouragement puts courage in my spouse.

53

I will

work to improve my communication skills.

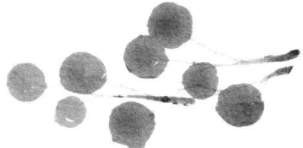

Learn from the experts you respect.

54

I will

limit the use of "you always" or "you never" when registering complaints.

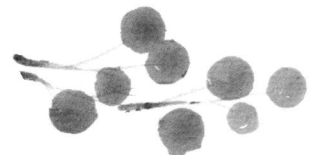

Extreme statements are seldom true. For example, rather than saying, "You never help with chores," say instead, "I need some help with the chores."

55

I will

choose to be a good listener.

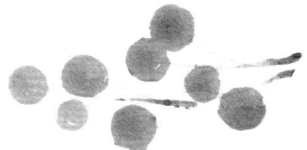

Give full eye contact; listen without interruption. Your spouse will feel more understood and affirmed.

56

I will

try not to take every cross word personally.

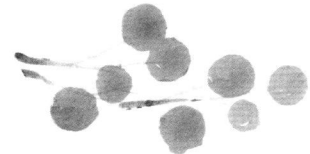

Sometimes, your spouse just needs to vent.

57

I will

stick to the subject and refrain from irrelevant and prior issues during disagreements.

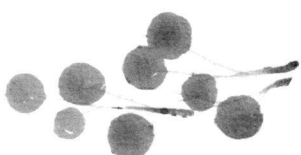

Attack the problem, rather than each other.

58

I will

share my deepest needs with my spouse.

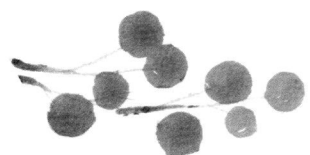

How can your spouse attempt to fulfill your needs if you haven't figured them out and expressed them directly?

59

I will

be aware that if I always have to be right, then I may have a control problem.

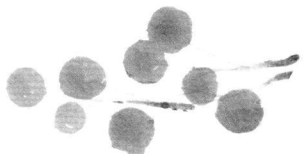

No one, including yourself, is perfect.

60

I will

refrain from complaining to my family about my spouse.

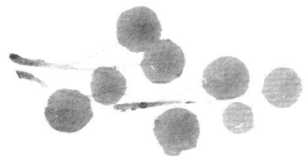

It's harder for them to forgive and forget.

61

I will

control my tongue.

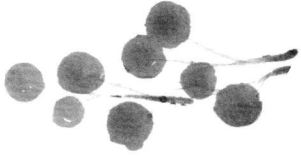

To avoid saying hurtful or careless words, close your mouth, take a deep breath, count to ten, or leave the room to cool down.

62

I will

say, "Thank you," and, "I appreciate…" as often as possible.

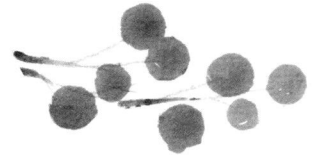

A spirit of gratitude benefits you both.

63

I will

realize that sulking and holding grudges hurts our relationship.

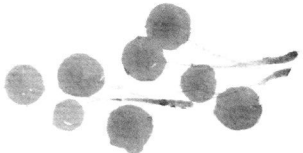

Pouting and withdrawing is not only a waste of time, it delays forgiveness.

64

I will

compliment the behavior I want to encourage in my spouse.

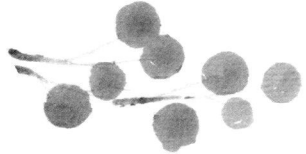

This is much more effective than nagging or complaining.

65

I will

forgive my spouse and settle differences as quickly as possible.

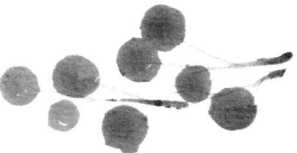

Holding a grudge without offering to resolve the issue hurts you and your spouse.

66

I will

realize that asking, "Will you forgive me?" is an important sequel to, "I am sorry."

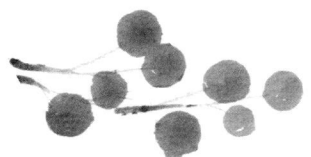

Asking and accepting forgiveness helps you both move forward.

67

I will

understand that my heart can be more teachable after being humbled.

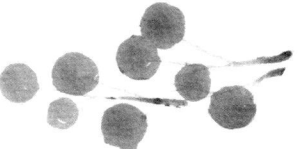

Failures can be teaching moments that promote growth.

68

I will

learn to negotiate a problem issue.

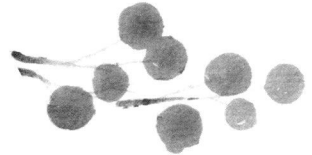

Be open to the other's point of view by communicating calmly, candidly, and clearly.

69

I will

tell the truth.

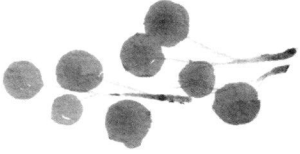

Lies have feet; they will follow you around.

70

I will

remember that mean-spirited words wound deeply.

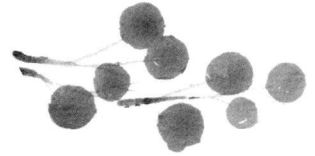

Hurtful words can never be taken back and can be replayed in your spouse's mind for years to come.

71

I will

learn to calmly express my concerns rather than fume silently or simply expect to be understood.

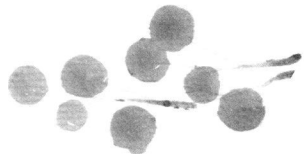

Saying, for example, "I just need some space right now," or, "I need some attention," can get results in a non-threatening way.

72

I will

recognize that it takes two to battle and take full responsibility for how I respond during disagreements.

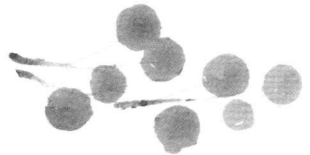

Even if "your spouse started it," there is no excuse for inappropriate language or behavior.

73

I will

allow my spouse to decompress from the day's work before major discussions.

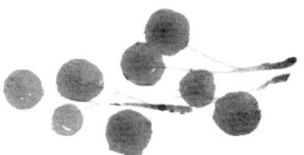

A relaxed spouse is usually more open and receptive.

74

I will

use loving, non-verbal communication often.

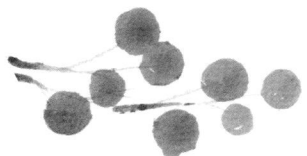

Loving eye contact, holding hands,
and hugs and kisses speak volumes.

75

I will

postpone important late night discussions until the morning.

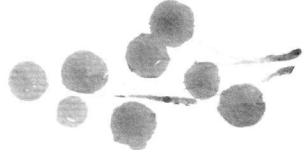

Timing is important. Things always look better when you are physically and mentally alert.

76

I will

realize that nagging will seldom create change in my spouse.

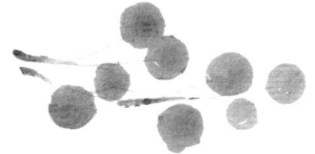

Nagging is usually counterproductive.

77

I will

learn to be more descriptive in my expressions of "I love you."

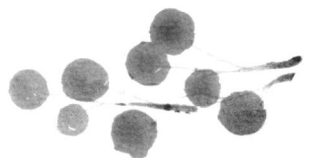

Consider, "I love the way…,"
"I love your…," "I appreciate…,"
"I am grateful for your…"

78

I will

respect my spouse's opinion, even if I disagree.

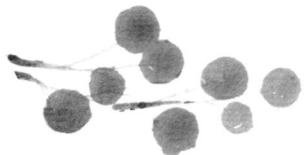

Sometimes, agreeing to disagree is the best way to resolve the situation.

79

I will

ask my spouse, "Is there something I can do (or not do) to make you feel more loved?"

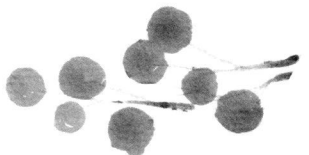

Sometimes the smallest change in habit or behavior can make a world of difference to your spouse.

80

I will

try to understand the reason for my spouse's anger or hostility.

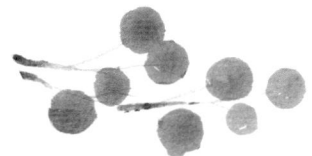

Knowing that anger can stem from hurt, fear, jealousy, resentment, fatigue, or depression will cause you to be more compassionate.

81

I will

keep a healthy sense of humor in our relationship.

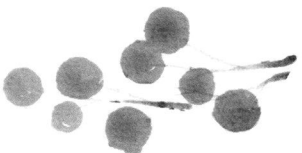

Laughter can be the best medicine.

Intimacy

82

I will

realize that loving, physical intimacy is the by-product of a loving relationship.

True intimacy comes from a connection of heart, mind, and soul.

83

I will

understand that intimacy in marriage is a gift designed by God.

It is meant not only for procreation, but for your delight.

84

I will

flee from the first thought of sexual temptation.

Choose social and work environments that will shield you from temptation. This includes not viewing pornography.

85

I will

have realistic expectations for our sexual intimacy.

There cannot be fireworks every time. You are two individuals with different expectations, moods, and hormone levels.

86

I will

find out what kind of date my spouse enjoys most.

Take turns doing what each partner enjoys. One person may like a sporting event, while the other prefers dinner or a movie.

87

I will

learn about the
differences between a man
and a woman's physical
and emotional needs
in intimacy.

Seek reliable resources rather than
advice from the trendy sources.

88

I will

keep flirtation, courtship, and spontaneity alive in my marriage.

It helps to maintain the manners and grooming habits that you practiced during courtship. (And please flirt only with your spouse.)

89

I will

make an effort to go to bed at the same time as my spouse in order to make time for romance.

Prioritizing down time together by putting down a book or turning off devices can sometimes speak volumes.

90

I will

express, "I'm thinking of you," with calls, gifts, or handwritten notes when it is not expected.

Don't limit yourself to the greeting card company's calendar to express your love.

91

I will

design our bedroom to be a romantic, soothing haven.

Exercise equipment, a TV, a computer, or an ironing board in full view can be distractions.

92

I will

acknowledge my spouse at the end of their workday.

When you stop what you are doing to welcome your spouse, you are saying, "I am happy to see you. I'm glad you're home."

93

I will

make time for intimacy.

Scheduling private time demonstrates commitment and can create anticipation.

94

I will

ask my spouse which personality traits were attractive during our courtship and keep those attributes alive.

Working with what you already have is easier than creating something new.

95

I will

learn what initiates the desire for intimacy in my spouse.

Intimacy will be enhanced when you fulfill your spouse's needs before you reach the bedroom.

96

I will

make physical and emotional fidelity to my spouse a lifelong goal.

Affairs usually begin with unmet emotional or physical needs.

97

I will

take turns being the initiator of intimacy.

It feels special to be desired.

98

I will

consider that I don't necessarily have to be in the mood as long as I am willing to be in the mood.

Once the loving begins, the mood will often follow.

99

I will

be a generous lover.

Mutual enjoyment should be your goal.

100

Finally, have a realistic expectation for putting these, "I Wills" into practice.

Marriage, like life, is taking one day at a time. Be patient with one another and yourself. Keep trying!

Blessings,
Lissa

Notes

Notes

Notes

Notes

Notes

Notes

Acknowledgments

To Randy, my chief editor and supporter, who joined me in believing our marriage could improve with work. Thank you for your loving commitment and faithfulness.

To Lauren and Walt, Randall and Ali, for your valuable editing and feedback. I love watching you prioritize your own marriages and adding your own "I Wills." Our grandchildren will flourish.

To Carroll and Sinclair for your patience and hard work for incorporating my vision for this second edition into reality.

To all my "unique unrepeatables," the amazing people who generously listened, shared ideas, typed, edited, gave input on covers and fonts, and are praying that this compiled wisdom and advice will help everyone who wants to work to strengthen their relationships.

In memory of our parents, Pat and D.A. Noel and Elmire and Foster Johns, who modeled many of these "I wills" during their respective seventy-six years of marriage.

Lastly, to my mentors – authors, preachers, teachers, encouragers, counselors, speakers, role models, and God's word that challenged me to work to put love into action and pass it on to future generations.

I am forever grateful.

A Note About the Cover

The principles of *One Hundred "I Wills" After You Say "I Do"* began with my parents, who were married seventy-six years.

For most of their life, they shared a deep love for nature. They gardened and built beds for flowers and vegetables. My dad's 9 to 5 job gave him the time to be a hands-on husband and father, as well as the designer and builder of all their landscaping plans.

Years ago, he used leftover concrete from a project to fashion the heart pictured here. He carved his and my mother's initials into the heart. This token of love was placed in the garden and was carried into future gardens, as was their commitment to nourish and serve each other.

My parents also had a photograph in their kitchen of two birds perched on the same tree branch. For me, those birds represented my parents looking out to the future in the same direction, through good times and bad. This steadfastness is one of the qualities it takes to finish strong in the journey of life.

You will find both of these elements, the heart and the birds, reflected on the cover of this book.

Thank you, Momma and Daddy.